C000017102

Illustrations copyright © 1998
C. James Frazier
Licensed by Wild Apple Licensing

Book design by Arlene Greco

Text Copyright © 1998
Peter Pauper Press, Inc.
202 Mamaroneck Avenue
White Plains, NY 10601
All rights reserved
ISBN 0-88088-383-9
Printed in China
7 6 5 4

Contents

Motherhood

Being a mother not
only takes time, but also
requires generous amounts
of faith and courage.

Once in a while,
give yourself permission
to pamper yourself.
A refreshed woman
is a happy mother.

When you speak softly,
you are more apt
to be heard.

A sense of humor
can turn a drama
into a comedy.

Beyond all lessons, beyond the model she provided, my mother gave me a parent's ultimate gift: She made me feel lovable and good. She paid attention; she listened; she remembered what I said. She did not think me perfect, but she accepted me, without qualification.

Fredelle Maynard

Children thirst to hear where they came from . . . they need to know that they were desired, that their birth was a wonder, and that they were always the object of love and care.

Marcelle Clements

I always wanted children, but not until they were actually part of my life did I realize that I could love that fiercely, or get that angry. Even when the kids were very little, I always found them fascinating people.

Cokie Roberts

Somewhere along the line of
development we discover what
we really are, and then we make
our real decision for which
we are responsible. Make that
decision primarily for yourself
because you can never live
anyone else's life, not even your
child's. The influence you exert
is through your own life and
what you become yourself.

Eleanor Roosevelt

*B*abies don't come with directions on the back or batteries that can be removed. Motherhood is twenty-four hours a day, seven days a week. You can't "leave the office."

Pat Schroeder

*E*very mother is like Moses.
She does not enter the
promised land. She prepares
a world she will not see.

Pope Paul VI

Motherhood was a scary, unknown thing, and work was familiar and secure. Work gave me more esteem as a mom. I thought, Okay, I can handle my job. Surely I can handle being this precious little girl's mom.

Leeza Gibbons

Motherhood is a
profession by itself,
just like school teaching
and lecturing.

Ida B. Wells

I cannot forget my mother.
Though not as sturdy as others,
she is my bridge. When I needed
to get across, she steadied
herself long enough for me
to run across safely.

Renita Weems

Every person needs recognition. It is expressed cogently by the child who says, "Mother, let's play darts. I'll throw the darts and you say, 'wonderful.'"

M. Dale Baugham

Whatever you would have
your children become, strive
to exhibit in your own lives
and conversation.

Lydia H. Sigourney

If a child lives with
approval, he learns to
live with himself.

Dorothy Law Nolte

She gives me good advice
all the time. Her instincts
are so incredible.

Swoosie Kurtz

And for the three magic gifts
I needed to escape the poverty
of my hometown, I thank my
mother, who gave me a sewing
machine, a typewriter, and
a suitcase. . . .

Alice Walker

I am a mother myself,
so why did it take me 35 years
to understand that mothers
aren't perfect?

Joyce Maynard

*A*nd maybe it's time
we admitted that a lot of
the traits—good and bad—
we blame on Mom would be
better attributed to life.

Sara Nelson

*M*y mother took for her motto in the training of her children the saying of some distinguished man: "Fill the measure with wheat and there will be no room for the chaff."

Maria Sanford

The most important thing a
mother can do to promote
her child's future welfare is
modeling a happy, fulfilled
person—somebody who is
taking care of her own needs,
who's happy, who's playful,
who's creative.

Lois Gobrecht

A mother's eyes may chastise,
or question, or show concern,
but they must always say,
"I love you."

The proverb, "Out of sight,
out of mind," never applies
to a mother's relationship
with her child.

Oh, to be only half as wonderful as my child thought I was when he was small, and only half as stupid as my teenager now thinks I am.

Rebecca Richards

Maybe I've been put on earth
to be an ordinary person.
Not to do anything great,
but to do something small
that involves great love.

Adoptive Mother

Stress

When life is full
of frustrations,
remember to unburden
your soul to a friend.

Take one step at a time;
before you know it,
you will have climbed to
the top, overcoming
many an obstacle.

When the stresses and
strains of everyday life feel
overwhelming, hug your child.
You will be embracing all that
is good in the world.

Meet the challenge of change
with joy rather than fear.
Anxiety causes a heavy burden,
while joy lifts the human spirit.

Dear Mother:
I'm all right.
Stop worrying about me.

Egyptian letter, 2000 BC

*I*t seems to me at times as if the weight of responsibility connected with these little immortal beings would prove too much for me—am I doing what's right? Am I doing enough? Am I not doing too much?

Abigail Alcott

Surrendering to
motherhood means
surrendering to interruption.

Erica Jong

I praise *casualness.* It seems to me the rarest of virtues. It is useful enough when children are small. It is important to the point of necessity when they are adolescents.

Phyllis McGinley

Smart mothers know that
tantrums and cross words will,
from time to time, cloud the
sunny experiences we want for
our children. So when nerves
get frazzled, these mothers step
back, take a breather and bank
on the most important yet
simplest guidelines of all:
Just love them.

Sue Woodman

A woman who can
cope with the terrible twos
can cope with anything.

Judith Clabes

The quickest way
for a mother to get a child's
attention is to sit down
and answer the telephone.

Ginny Unser

I do believe I am a good
mother. I try to stay out of
my children's way. I try to give
them information because
I worry, but you can't figure out
all their problems for them.
You can only assist.

Debbie Reynolds

Responsibility

A tiny seed grows into a plant
which flowers when nurtured
with care and love.

*L*ove your children with all your hearts, love them enough to discipline them before it is too late. . . . praise them for important things, even if you have to stretch them a bit. Praise them a lot. They live on it like bread and butter and they need it more . . .

Lavina Christensen Fugal,
Mother of the Year, 1995

52

Mother showed me and the world that no matter where you are born, to whom and under what conditions, you can achieve anything you want. She walked with kings, queens and presidents and never lost the human touch.

Dee Dee Bellson,
daughter of Pearl Bailey

My earliest memories were of my mother writing her Ph.D. dissertation and taking care of my brother and myself. Her emphasis on education, social responsibility, and the importance of a woman's fulfilling herself have shaped my outlook fundamentally and irrevocably.

Congresswoman Elizabeth Holtzman

And one of the things we need to do as parents is to let our children handle their failures— be there to support them, but let them handle the disappointing moments. Because that's how they build the ability to go out on their own and face obstacles.

Gray Whitestone,
mother of Miss America,
Heather Whitestone

More than in any other human relationship, overwhelmingly more, motherhood means being instantly interruptible, responsive, responsible.

Tillie Olsen

Cleaning your house while your
kids are still growing is like
shoveling the walk before
it stops snowing.

Phyllis Diller

A suburban mother's role
is to deliver children
obstetrically once, and
by car forever after.

Peter de Vries

I hope they are still making
women like my Momma.
She always told me to do the
right thing, to have pride
in myself—and that a good
name is better than money.

Joe Louis

*P*arenthood is the art
of bringing children up without
putting them down.

Anonymous

Children are likely to
live up to what you believe
of them.

Lady Bird Johnson

Nobody's Perfect

Make a list of your priorities.
Remember you can do only
one thing at a time.

I think every working mom goes through the times when you feel that if you weren't working perhaps you'd be giving them a little more. I've always believed the quality of the time is so much more important than the quantity.

Jackie Zeman

At work, you think of the
children you have left at home.
At home, you think of the
work you've left unfinished.

Golda Meir

Self Reliance

Being a mother, it seems, is a process of constantly adapting to the needs of your child while also changing and growing as a person in your own right.

A mother is not a person
to lean on but a person to make
leaning unnecessary.

Dorothy Canfield Fisher

My ultimate goal always was to have a family. Now that's come true. Now my goal is to teach my children how to grow up with love and discipline.

Vanna White

Family

I know why families were
created, with all their
imperfections. They humanize
you. They are made to make you
forget yourself occasionally,
so that the beautiful balance of
life is not destroyed.

Anaïs Nin

I often think back to my childhood with four siblings, and wonder: How did my mother ever manage to bring such amazing order to our hectic lives? She made it a top priority.

Jeanne Brooks-Gunn, Ph.D.

I used to try to shape my family in the image of the family I grew up in. But my mom helped me see things differently. She told me, "You have to create your own family. You have to come up with a new model that works for you."

Ann Vaaler

When my mother had to
get dinner for eight she'd just
make enough for sixteen
and only serve half.

Gracie Allen

Mother was of royal African
blood, of a tribe ruled by
matriarchs. . . . Throughout all
her bitter years of slavery she
had managed to preserve
a queenlike dignity. She
supervised all the business
of the family.

Mary McLeod Bethune

*A*s she supplies the
affection and care that make a
contented home, each mother
is strengthening the individuals
within her own circle as well
as in the nation.

Earl E. Chanley

I saw her working, being the emotional and spiritual leader in our family. She had almost a fanatical emphasis on education. We got encyclopedias, and she struggled to make those payments. She kept saying, "I don't care what you do, but be the best at it."

Judge Sonia Sotomayor